Soho Theatre and Damsel Productions
present

# by Phoebe Eclair-Powell

*Fury* received its world premiere on 5 July 2016
at Soho Theatre, London

# FURY

**by Phoebe Eclair-Powell**

## CAST

| | |
|---|---|
| **Sam** | Sarah Ridgeway |
| **Tom** | Alex Austin |
| **Woman** | Naana Agyei-Ampadu |
| **Man** | Daniel Kendrick |
| **Fury** | Anita-Joy Uwajeh |

## CREATIVE TEAM

| | |
|---|---|
| **Director** | Hannah Hauer-King |
| **Designer** | Anna Reid |
| **Lighting Designer** | Natasha Chivers |
| **Music and Sound** | Nathan Klein |
| **Casting Director** | Nadine Rennie CDG |
| **Assistant Director** | Avigail Tlalim |
| **Production Manager** | Sarah Cowan |
| **Stage Manager** | Rike Berg |

# BIOGRAPHIES

### SARAH RIDGEWAY (SAM)

Theatre credits include: *Forget Me Not* (Bush); *Harrogate* (HighTide); *The Cherry Orchard* (Young Vic); Viola in *Twelfth Night* (Regent's Park Open Air Theatre); *Candide, A Mad World, My Masters, Titus Andronicus, Days of Significance* (RSC); *The Accrington Pals, You Can't Take It With You* (Royal Exchange); *Sucker Punch* (Royal Court); *Comedy of Errors* (Shakespeare's Globe); *A Taste of Honey* (Salisbury Playhouse); Juliet in *Romeo and Juliet* (Northern Broadsides).

Television credits include: *Holby City, Kerry & Lu's Taster, EastEnders, Doctors* (BBC); *The Making of a Lady, Miss Marple* (ITV); *Dark Matters* (Discovery Channel); *Call the Midwife* (Neal Street Productions); *Satisfaction* (Eat Me Productions); *The Suspicions of Mr Whicher* (Hat Trick Productions); *Crimson Petal and the White* (Origin Pictures); *The Bill* (Talkback Thames).

### ALEX AUSTIN (TOM)

Theatre credits include: Jay in *Barbarians* (Bad Physics/Young Vic); *The Skriker* (Royal Exchange); *Henry V*, Fritz in *The Nutcracker, The Man with the Disturbingly Smelly Foot* (Unicorn); Hench in *Yen* (Royal Exchange/Royal Court); *Idomeneus* (Gate); *Pigeons* (Royal Court); *Hope Light and Nowhere* (Suba Das Company/Underbelly); *HMP Feltham Project* (Synergy); *Ryan Gander: Locked Room Scenario* (Artsangel); *Life in my Shoes* (Body & Soul Charity); *My City* (Almeida); *Encourage the Others* (Almeida Young Friends); *We Will Rock You!* (CANDI Youth Theatre); *Platform* (Old Vic New Voices).

Film and television credits include: *Sherlock* (Hartswood); *The Interceptor, New Tricks, The Musketeers, Holby City* (BBC); *Legacy* (Legacy Films); *The Christmas Candle* (Pinewood Films); *The Hooligan Factory* (Altitude HF Ltd); *The World's End* (Blank Pictures Ltd); *Misfits* (Clerkenwell Films); *The Swarm* (Stray Bear Productions).

### NAANA AGYEI-AMPADU (WOMAN)

Theatre credits include: *I Want My Hat Back, The Amen Corner, Caroline, or Change* (National Theatre); *The Oresteia, Measure for Measure, The Frontline* (Shakespeare's Globe); *Made in Dagenham* (Adelphi); *Feast, Been So Long* (Young Vic); *Little Shop of Horrors* (New Wolsey); *Avenue Q* (Noël Coward).

Television credits include: *Cuffs* (Tiger Aspect for BBC); *The Future Wags of Great Britain* (Channel 4).

### DANIEL KENDRICK (MAN)

Daniel trained at Mountview Academy of Theatre Arts.

Theatre credits include: *So Here We Are* (Royal Exchange/HighTide Festival); *Our Town* (Almeida); *If You Don't Let Us Dream, We Won't Let You Sleep, Ding Dong the Wicked, Vera, Vera, Vera* (Royal Court); *Rosie and Jim* (Mobculture); *Chapel Street* (Old Red Lion/Liverpool Playhouse); *Coalition* (Theatre503).

Film and television credits include: *#Us and Them* (Into the Woods); *Offender* (Gunslinger Films); *Lovebite* (Ecosse Films); *Call the Midwife* (Neal Street Productions); *Black Mirror* (Channel 4); *Ripper Street* (Tiger Aspect for BBC); *Our World War* (BBC3); *Mr Selfridge* (ITV); *Run* (Channel 4); *EastEnders* (BBC).

### ANITA-JOY UWAJEH (FURY)

Theatre credits include: *We Wait in Joyful Hope* (Theatre503); *Othello* (Smooth Faced Gents, Edinburgh Festival); *Titus Andronicus* (Smooth Faced Gents, Greenwich); *Gone Too Far, A Day at the Racists, Lady From the Sea, Ivanov, Threesome, Twelfth Night, The White Devil, Iphigenia in Aulis* (Drama Centre); *Bow Down* (The Opera Group); *Every Human Creature* (Southwark Playhouse Young Company).

Film credits include: *Agent 47* (Fox). Television credits include: *Lucky Man* (Carnival for Sky 1); *Not Safe for Work* (Clerkenwell Films for Channel 4); *Transporter* (Atlantique Productions).

**PHOEBE ECLAIR-POWELL (WRITER)**

Phoebe is a writer from South-East London. She is the 2016 Writer-in-Residence at Soho Theatre. *Fury* was a finalist for the 2015 Verity Bargate Award and won the Soho Theatre Young Writers' Award.

Her other plays include: *Epic Love and Pop Songs* (Pleasance, Edinburgh); *WINK* (Tara Finney/Theatre503); *One Under* (Pleasance Below); *Mrs Spine* (OUTLINES at the Old Red Lion); *Bangin' Wolves* (Courting Drama at the Bush Upstairs, published by Playdead Press, later with Poleroid Theatre for Wilderness Festival); two Rapid Write Response pieces, *Coal Eaters* and *Glass Hands* (Theatre503); *The Box* (Theatre Delicatessen SPACED festival and Latitude Festival); *Elephant and My Castle* (SALT Theatre at Southwark Playhouse); *CARE* (Miniaturists at the Arcola).

**HANNAH HAUER-KING (DIRECTOR)**

Hannah is artistic director and co-founder of Damsel Productions. She recently acted as resident AD at Soho Theatre, after working in Washington DC for Nomadic Theatre and graduating from Georgetown University with a degree in Performing Arts.

Recent work includes: *Brute* (Soho); *Clay* (Pleasance); *Dry Land* (Jermyn Street); *PLAY* (Old Red Lion); *When I Met Rosie* (Pleasance/The Space), *pool (no water)* (Nomadic Theatre, DC); *Spring Awakening* (M&B Theatre, Washington DC) and assistant on *Radiant Vermin* (Soho); *Symphony* (Soho/Edinburgh Fringe); *Daytona* (Theatre Royal Haymarket). She is currently also working as a theatre, cabaret and comedy programmer for United Music.

**ANNA REID (DESIGNER)**

Anna is a set and costume designer based in London, a graduate of Wimbledon College of Art, and is the associate designer for Damsel Productions.

Designer credits include: *For Those Who Cry When They Hear the Foxes Scream* (Tristan Bates); *Tape* (The Drayton Arms); *Brute* (Soho); *Primadonna* (Waterloo Vaults); *Dottir* (The Courtyard); *Dry Land* (Jermyn Street); *Bruises* (Tabard); *SKINT* (Waterloo Vaults); *Arthur's World* (Bush); *Hippolytos* (Victoria and Albert Museum); *Fierce* (Camden People's Theatre); *Fifth Column* (Waterloo Vaults); *Hamlet* (Riverside Studios); *Crossing the Line* (Maltings, St Albans); *The Spanish Tragedy* (King's College Chapel); *more* (The Corpus Playrooms); *Macbeth* (The ADC Theatre and various US venues).

Upcoming credits include: *Jumpers for Goalposts* (Oldham Coliseum).

www.annareiddesign.com

## NATASHA CHIVERS (LIGHTING DESIGNER)

Natasha Chivers' work includes: *Sunset at the Villa Thalia* (National Theatre); *Strapless, Electric Counterpoint* (ROH); *Gravity Fatigue, Encore* (Sadler's Wells); *Oresteia* (2016 Olivier nomination, Best Lighting; Almeida/West End); *1984* (Headlong at the Almeida/West End/UK and international tours); *That Face* (Royal Court/West End); *Who Cares, Fireworks, Adler & Gibb, The Mistress Contract, Gastronauts, The Djinns of Eidgah* (Royal Court); *The Insatiable Inflatable Candylion, Mother Courage and Her Children, The Radicalisation of Bradley Manning* (National Theatre Wales); *Praxis Makes Perfect* (Theatre Critics of Wales Award, Best Lighting; Neon Neon/National Theatre Wales); *Macbeth* (also Broadway and tour of Japan); *27, The Wheel, Mary Stuart, The House of Bernard Alba, Home (Glasgow)* (National Theatre of Scotland); *Green Snake* (National Theatre of China); *Statement of Regret* (National Theatre); *Sunday in the Park with George* (Olivier Award for Best Lighting Design; West End); *The Wolves in the Walls* (National Theatre of Scotland/Improbable); *Othello, Dirty Wonderland, pool (no water), Tiny Dynamite, Peepshow, Hymns, Sell-Out* (Frantic Assembly); *The Four Fridas, Run!, Renaissance* (Greenwich + Docklands International Festivals); *Mesmerics, Metheus* (BalletBoyz The Talent/Linbury Studio); *Motor Show* (LIFT/Brighton Festival); *Electric Hotel* (Sadler's Wells/Fuel); *God's Garden for Arthur Pita* (ROH Linbury/tour); *Broken and Scattered* (Motionhouse). She won a Theatre Award UK for Best Design (with Lizzie Clachan) in 2011 for *Happy Days* (Sheffield Crucible).

www.natashachivers.co.uk


## NATHAN KLEIN (MUSIC AND SOUND)

Nathan Klein is a composer whose musical work has spanned from West End theatre to internationally released television series and feature films.

Composing music and designing sound for theatre, Nathan was nominated for an Off West End Award for his work on *How I Learned to Drive* (Southwark Playhouse). Other theatre credits include: *Before You Were Born* (Trafalgar Studios 2); *Dry Land* (Jermyn Street); *I and the Village* (Theatre503); *The Odyssey* (Nuffield). Past work for stage also includes the Oxford Playhouse, the Tokyo Metropolitan Arts Theatre, and Yvonne Arnaud Theatre. Composing for feature film and documentary includes: *Butterfly Kisses* (Blue Shadows Films/BBC Films/Film London); *Avanti!* (Abuelita Productions). As an orchestrator, credits include: *War and Peace* (BBC Wales/Weinstein Company); *Steve Jobs* (Universal Pictures); *Victoria* (ITV); *From the Land of the Moon* (Studio Canal).

www.nkcomposition.co.uk


## KITTY WORDSWORTH (PRODUCER FOR DAMSEL PRODUCTIONS)

Kitty is executive producer and co-founder of Damsel Productions.

After graduating from Sussex University in 2014, Kitty produced the Portobello Pantomime, *Peter Panto* (The Tabernacle, December 2014). Producer credits include: *Dry Land* (Jermyn Street); *Dick Whit* (The Tabernacle); *Brute* (Soho). Associate producer credits include: world premiere of Jonathan Guy Lewis's *A Level Playing Field* (Jermyn Street); the So and So Arts Club's Repertory Season, *Ever HopeFull*. Kitty also works part-time at Lee Menzies Ltd.

# LONDON'S MOST VIBRANT VENUE FOR NEW THEATRE, COMEDY AND CABARET

Soho Theatre is a major creator of new theatre, comedy and cabaret. Across our three different spaces we curate the finest live performance we can discover, develop and nurture. Soho Theatre works with theatre makers and companies in a variety of ways, from full producing of new plays, to co-producing new work, working with associate artists and presenting the best new emerging theatre companies that we can find.

We have numerous writers and theatre makers on attachment and under commission, six young writers and comedy groups and we read and see hundreds of shows a year – all in an effort to bring our audience work that amazes, moves and inspires.

'Soho Theatre was buzzing, and there were queues all over the building as audiences waited to go into one or other of the venue's spaces. [The audience] is so young, exuberant and clearly anticipating a good time.' Guardian

We attract over 170,000 audience members a year. We produced, co-produced or staged over forty new plays in the last twelve months.

Our social enterprise business model means that we maximise value from Arts Council and philanthropic funding; we actually contribute more to government in tax and NI than we receive in public funding.

**sohotheatre.com**

Keep up to date:
sohotheatre.com/mailing-list
facebook.com/sohotheatre
twitter.com/sohotheatre
youtube.com/sohotheatre

Registered Charity No: 267234

Soho Theatre, 21 Dean Street
London W1D 3NE
Admin 020 7287 5060
Box Office 020 7478 0100

Supported using public funding by
**ARTS COUNCIL ENGLAND**

# SUBMITTING YOUR WORK TO SOHO THEATRE

We make the very best entertaining, challenging, profound new work across a range of live performance genres.

We are the place where emerging and established writers conceive, develop and realise their work.

We want to push the form in a way that delights and inspires our audience.

There are no thematic, political or philosophical constraints and though we love to produce a writers' first play, we have no objection to your second, third or fiftieth.

**We are looking for unique and unheard voices – from all backgrounds, attitudes and places.**

**We want to make things you've never seen before.**

If you would like to submit a script to us please send it as a PDF or Word attachment to: **submissions@sohotheatre.com**

Your play will go directly to our Artistic team.

We consider every submission for production or for further development opportunities. Although there are a limited number of slots on our stages, we engage with writers throughout the year through workshops, readings, notes sessions and other opportunities.

# DEVELOPMENT AND DONORS

Soho Theatre is a charity and social enterprise. We are supported by Arts Council England and we put every £1 we make back into our work. Our supporters are key to our success and we are immensely grateful for their support. We would like to thank Soho Theatre Friends and Members as well as our supporters:

**Principal Supporters**
Nicholas Allott
Hani Farsi
Jack & Linda Keenan
Amelia & Neil Mendoza
Lady Susie Sainsbury
Carolyn Ward
Jennifer & Roger Wingate

**The Soho Circle**
Celia Atkin
Moyra Doyle
Stephen Garrett
Hedley & Fiona Goldberg
Jon Grant
Tim Macready
Suzanne Pirret

**Corporate Supporters**
Adnams Southwold
Bargate Murray
Bates Wells & Braithwaite
Cameron Mackintosh Ltd
EPIC Private Equity
Financial Express
Fosters
The Groucho Club
John Lewis Oxford Street
Latham & Watkins LLP
Lionsgate UK
The Nadler Hotel
Oberon Books Ltd
Overbury Leisure
Quo Vadis
Richmond Associates
Soho Estates
Soundcraft

**Trusts & Foundations**
The Andor Charitable Trust
The Austin and Hope Pilkington Charitable Trust
Backstage Trust
Bertha Foundation
Boris Karloff Charitable Foundation
Bruce Wake Charitable Trust

The Buzzacott Stuart Defries Memorial Fund
The Chapman Charitable Trust
The Charles Rifkind & Jonathan Levy Charitable Settlement
Cockayne – Grants for the Arts and The London Community Foundation
The Coutts Charitable Trust
The David and Elaine Potter Foundation
The D'Oyly Carte Charitable Trust
The Ernest Cook Trust
The Edward Harvist Trust
The 8th Earl of Sandwich Memorial Trust
The Eranda Foundation
Esmée Fairbairn Foundation
The Fenton Arts Trust
The Foundation for Sport and the Arts
The Foyle Foundation
The Goldsmiths' Company
Harold Hyam Wingate Foundation
Help A London Child
Hyde Park Place Estate Charity
The Ian Mactaggart Trust
The Idlewild Trust
John Ellerman Foundation
John Lewis Oxford Street Community Matters Scheme
John Lyon's Charity
The John Thaw Foundation
JP Getty Jnr Charitable Trust
The Kobler Trust

The Mackintosh Foundation
The Mohamed S. Farsi Foundation
The Peggy Ramsay Foundation
The Rose Foundation
The Royal Victoria Hall Foundation
St Giles-in-the-Fields and William Shelton Educational Charity
The St James's Piccadilly Charity
Teale Charitable Trust
The Theatres Trust
The Thistle Trust
Unity Theatre Charitable Trust
The Wolfson Foundation

**Soho Theatre Best Friends**
Matthew & Brooke Barzun
Nick Bowers
Prof Dr Niels Brabandt
Barbara Broccoli
Richard Collins
David and Beverly Cox
Miranda Curtis
Norma Heyman
Isobel & Michael Holland
Beatrice Hollond
David King
Lady Caroline Mactaggart
Hannah Pierce
Amy Ricker
Ian Ritchie & Jocelyne van den Bossche
Ann Stanton
Alex Vogel
Sian & Matthew Westerman
Mark Whiteley
Gary Wilder
Alexandra Williams
Hilary and Stuart Williams

# DAMSEL
## PRODUCTIONS

Damsel Productions was established in 2015 by **Hannah Hauer-King** and **Kitty Wordsworth** with the key aim of actively placing the female voice centre stage.

Our idea is simple: to bring together female theatre artists, directors and producers to breathe life into scripts written by women. Our productions aim to provoke, inspire, shock and, of course, entertain with true and honest representations of the female experience. We hope to engage and empower audiences who may generally shy away or feel excluded from the theatre experience.

In November 2015, we proudly presented our first production, the UK première of *Dry Land* by Ruby Rae Spiegel – an important coming-of-age story about abortion, sexuality, bodies, swimming, the often painful experience of being a teenager and an unlikely friendship put to the most extreme of tests. The production at Jermyn Street Theatre was a sell-out, receiving a great critical response, being described in the *Independent* as *"an auspicious debut for Damsel Productions, the ironically named and inspiring new company dedicated to putting provocative, true and honest aspects of female experience centre stage."*

In March 2016, we produced *Brute*, Izzy Tennyson's acclaimed one-woman show, at Soho Theatre. We couldn't be happier to be back at Soho Theatre so soon with *Fury*.

# DAMSEL
## PRODUCTIONS

* * * * * * * * * * * * * * * * * * * * * * * * * * * * * * * * * * * * * * * * * * * *

| | |
|---|---|
| Artistic Director and Co-Founder | **Hannah Hauer-King** |
| Executive Producer and Co-Founder | **Kitty Wordsworth** |
| Designer | **Anna Reid** |
| Associate Producer | **Zoe Weldon** |
| Associate Artist and Social Media | **Charlotte Hamblin** |

Thank you to our supporters and donors so far, without whom Damsel wouldn't be possible:

Nicholas Allott, Anonymous, Baker, Suzy Barry, Angela Bernstein and the Quercus Trust, Jonathan Blake, Jo Butler Dwyer, Ben Coleman, Bryony Coleman, Juliet Cowan, Alex Cruz, Miranda Davis, Andrew Dorman, Sophie Dowling, Jenny Eclair, Beatie Edney, The Hani Farsi Foundation, Lucy Flannery, Lady Antonia Fraser, Angharad George-Carey, Debra Hauer, Marc Hauer, Queenie Ingrams, Rebecca John, Jeremy King, Jonathan Margolis, Peter Moore, Sarita Moore, Deborah Orr, Bel Powley, Peter Raeburn, Nina Steiger, Tigerlily Taylor, Jenny Topper, Nellie Windsor-Clive, Cressida Wordsworth, Megan Wyler, Louisa Young.

* * * * * * * * * * * * * * * * * * * * * * * * * * * * * * * * * * * * * * * * * * * *

To get in touch, please email: **hello@damselproductions.co.uk**

Or visit: **damselproductions.co.uk**

Chat with us at: **@DamselProd**

# FURY

Phoebe Eclair-Powell

**Acknowledgements**

Thanks to:

Hannah Hauer-King for getting it – completely.

To Kitty Wordsworth for being a gem and all at Damsel Productions. To Nina Steiger for pushing me further, and to Deirdre O'Halloran and Joe Murphy for keeping me going. To Nadine Rennie for her spot-on genius. To all at Soho Theatre for being amazing, supportive and kind people – led by the amazing Steve Marmion. To Tanya Gould, Phil Porter and the brilliant Sarah Dickenson.

To Wally Jiago for being a mate and a great help in showing me the facts and figures, to Rebecca Harvey for telling me a thing or two about care. To Jess Waite for sharing her truth as hard as it was – you are a heroine. To Yasmin Joseph for the starting point – 'don't mug yerself'.

To those who helped me hear it for real and made it so – Sarah Ridgeway, Alex Austin, Naana Agyei-Ampadu, Daniel Kendrick, Anita-Joy Uwajeh, Lizzy Watts, Jonny Holden, Lucy Thackeray, Greg Barnett, and Tom Shepherd.

To those who bought it to life with their talent – Anna Reid, Nathan Klein, Natasha Chivers, Avigail Tlalim, Rike Berg, and The Other Richard boys.

Thanks to Jamie Jackson – always.

Thanks to Ikenna Obiekwe who told me there were 'three sides'.

To Tristram Bawtree for your kindness and support with that hard-to-find ending. And to my parents, who, once again, bore the brunt of the bad times and helped me celebrate the good. Especially my mum – who is my best and most trusted confidante.

*P. E-P.*

## Note on Play

The Chorus act like every Greek chorus should – they ask us to
bear witness. But this Chorus also manipulates our understanding
of the story unravelling before us. They shape our idea of Sam
and our sense of judgement. They are a three-headed hydra –
with slight differences in allegiance. Fury is more on Sam's side,
Man is on the fence – sometimes playful, sometimes vengeful –
and Woman is the least sympathetic – perhaps she has seen this
all before and she's tired of it. When the Chorus speak they take
over – they infiltrate the stage and enhance the theatrical journey.
They should be supported by music and underscore – they take us
out of naturalism and into something far more heightened.

The Chorus lines are written as one big poem, a long-running,
free-flowing spoken-word piece. Future productions should feel
free to reallocate the lines according to their vision of the Chorus.
I would be very happy for people to have more than three Chorus
members – in fact, I would love to see a version of this play with
hundreds of Chorus! The Chorus should hardly pause for breath –
they are fighting to get this story out and it is relentless, an assault
on the audience.

The Chorus will sing versions of various songs, mostly 'Get Free'
by Major Lazer, featuring Amber. They might need a loop pedal
and some instruments – microphones and the like. A brilliant
sound person can use the songs to create soundscapes, perhaps
from Sam's environment, but the lyrics are important. Tom uses
music as a weapon. We use music to take us far away. Whilst the
Chorus sing, perhaps Sam and Tom dance, perhaps they dance
really, really hard. The Chorus want us to witness, they also want
to take charge of who feels what. Our sympathies twist and turn –
Sam is our tragic hero; she makes many mistakes. Who can
blame her...

**Characters**

SAM, *mother*
TOM, *monster*

CHORUS
WOMAN (W), *plays* CLIENT/BOSS/OFFICER 1
MAN (M), *plays* ROB/POLICE/OFFICER 2
FURY (F), *plays* FRIEND/OFFICER 3

*This is one way of sharing the parts, you may find your own, or find another way of allocating the lines – all is up to you.*

*This text went to press before the end of rehearsals and so may differ slightly from the play as performed.*

CHORUS *sing the first verse and refrain of 'Get Free' by Major Lazer, featuring Amber.*

| | |
|---|---|
| W | Sam is a single mother. |
| F | She is also a Londoner in the truest sense of the word – |
| M | South of the river before you ask. |
| W | And she lives in a flat that used to be for people like her, but now squeezes the rich and the confused of Peckham, as the bankers roll in. |
| M | The time is now, or really 2017, the moment when they decided that if two tipped into three they wouldn't be able to sustain that figure. That child won't exist – it will just have to do without. |
| F | And thousands will have to pack up and leave because they're just not worth it. |
| M | Back to Sam |
| W | We have to introduce our hero, our woman of the hour. |
| F | The hour that you will spend here watching her. |
| W | You can imagine her how you will. |
| M | We imagined her like this – |
| W | And we will tear her down together |
| F | As we all do |
| M | All day |
| W | Every day. |
| M | This is the bit where I tell you she stole a golden fleece, shagged a relative, murdered her father or made a pact with a god. |

| | |
|---|---|
| F | But our Sam didn't do any of those things |
| | Our Sam has lived a normal life, |
| M | as we all have. |
| W | Our Sam was born, she went to school, she met a boy called Rob and they had two kids too soon |
| M | But now Rob is married to a vain young woman called Carly, though Carly would laugh and say she's not a woman, not yet, she's not ready. |
| F | But no one is really ready for anything. |
| W | Sam doesn't know her mother. |
| M | Her father is dead. |
| W | That makes her slightly more unusual |
| | In the statistical sense. |
| | *The* CHORUS *start to hum.* |
| M | Now is the time to play music |
| | Loud music. |
| | CHORUS *sing the first and second refrain of 'Get Free' – loud.* |
| TOM | Sorry about the noise. |
| SAM | Alright. |
| | I'd love to play loud music trust me, but they need – |
| | They have small ears you know – wake up all the time. |
| | You need to – |
| | Just be mindful. |
| | Not being like your mum an' all. |
| TOM | No. |

| | |
|---|---|
| SAM | Have you got anything to smoke? |
| | Just I smelt it before. |
| TOM | I'm not the one who – |
| SAM | Oh right. |
| | He coming back later or… |
| TOM | Probably not. |
| | It's a Saturday night. |
| SAM | Oh yeah. |
| | Yeah it is. |
| | You not out then? |
| TOM | Got a paper / part of my degree course. |
| SAM | You got that anxiety disorder, don't like going out, being around people – |
| | Too many people make you think you gunna wet yourself or do a shit or something – |
| TOM | No, no it's fine, I'm fine actually. |
| | So if you don't – |
| SAM | Yeah, yeah. |
| | Oh wow you guys have a big telly. |
| | Got any sort of Netflix on there? |
| TOM | Sky. |
| | Dave's dad works for – so we… |
| SAM | Can we come and watch cartoons sometimes? |
| | Could you do that? |
| | Let us in on Saturday mornings? |
| | For a treat. |
| | I could make you all breakfast or something. |
| TOM | Are you okay? |

| SAM | Fine, why you ask? |
|-----|--------------------|
|     | Sure he's not coming back? |
| TOM | I could have a drink if you wanted a drink? |
| SAM | No thanks, drank enough last night. |
| TOM | Right. |
| SAM | Right. |
|     | Could I have a slice of toast? |
| TOM | Um okay yeah. |
|     | Yeah sure, um, I mean, it's not, well it's actually Becca's so, um, I might – |
| SAM | What's yours then? |
| TOM | Can of Stella, and some Frosties. |
|     | *She indicates the Frosties. He hands over the box.* |
|     | But I haven't got any um... milk. |
|     | SAM *is already shovelling the dry cereal into her mouth.* |
| SAM | How come you guys living in council accommodation? |
| TOM | Um we rent it – I don't really know. |
|     | They got it off Zoopla, or one of them... websites. |
| SAM | Right. |
|     | So you work then? |
| TOM | No I'm still on my MA so... |
|     | Dave and Becca are doing BAs though. |
| SAM | Becca your girlfriend, or just the one you want to shag a bit? |
| TOM | One I want to shag to be honest. |

| | |
|---|---|
| SAM | She's not that good looking really though is she. |
| | … |
| | Can I watch telly with my Frosties? |
| TOM | Um, I sort of need to – |
| SAM | I can just watch like ten minutes. |
| | Telly bit fuckin' slow if you / ask |
| TOM | Sorry I can't um… maybe you should, I think I hear crying. |
| | CHORUS *start to hum*. |
| SAM | I don't. |
| TOM | No I think, maybe one of your boys – |
| SAM | I don't think – |
| TOM | Really because / I think |
| SAM | Yes… yes I hear them. |

*Chorus*

| | |
|---|---|
| W | When Sam was nineteen she pushed a little boy, |
| F | a tiny soul |
| W | into the world of a hospital bed. |
| F | And the paper sheets were ripped with blood and sweat and the legs of her and her baby trembled. |
| W | And things slid and hearts moved to rhythms preordained. |
| M | All this and we can get somewhere to live is just one tiny thought that crossed her terrified and lonely brain and Rob held her hand and grinned. |

| | |
|---|---|
| F | And she thought – well at least he will keep me safe, even if this crying thing scares the life out of me. |
| W | I can put it in your large hands. |
| M | Surely you will do this for me. |
| F | Keep a hold of this for me please. |

| | |
|---|---|
| SAM | Sh, shush, shush please shh. |
| CLIENT (W) | Oh it's you again – you didn't do a very good job last time, the skirting boards. |
| | I could just see they weren't clean. |
| | Would you mind doing it properly – please. |
| SAM | Yeah sure, sorry, the agency said. They already ticked me off, so you don't have to. |
| CLIENT | No need to be rude, really. |
| SAM | I wasn't being... I've bought one of my little boys with me. He wasn't feeling up to nursery. He can just sit in a corner, can't he? |
| CLIENT | Sorry did he come last time? Only we noticed some food had gone... missing. |
| | Just some of our food wasn't where it should've been in the fridge and I think – |
| SAM | No, no I don't know anything about / that, honestly. |
| CLIENT | I think we might give it a miss this week, actually, if you don't mind. Can you get off my doorstep. Please. |
| SAM | Are you being serious. Really? Really? |
| TOM | Hello. |
| | I own toast this time, if you wanted some. |

SAM        No thanks, you still got that can of Stella?

           Jesus Christ.

           Look at this place.

TOM        Yeah sorry we all get a bit messy.

           Thinking of getting a cleaner.

SAM        But it's a flat.

           A small flat.

TOM        Yeah but we just don't have time you know –

           And you can get really cheap ones,
           companies –

SAM        Right yeah.

           I clean.

TOM        Oh right.

SAM        I'm not doing your flat, before you ask.
           I wouldn't do your flat.

TOM        I didn't ask you to, sorry – can I help you
           with something?

SAM        The boys are at their dad's.

TOM        That's... uh –

SAM        So you in again by yourself?

TOM        No Becca's home.

           But in her room with her –

SAM        Her boyfriend.

           Rough.

           Not listening in?

           Sorry.

TOM        I was going out actually.

SAM        Can I come?

*Chorus*

| | |
|---|---|
| W | When Sam was twenty-one she pushed so hard for her other son that her life played out in streams against her eyeballs and the nurse squeezed her hand so tight as if to pull her back from whatever light was calling for her. |
| F | She told her to hold on, please, you're not leaving yet, you have to see him breathe and she did. |
| | And she sees him every day and sometimes she wishes she could stop them both. |
| M | Rob arrived late, because Carly had cried and cried and told him to sort out his life and that's why the nurse was holding her hand |
| W | And not him. |
| M | Not his large hands this time. |
| | |
| SAM | Mine's a pint. |
| TOM | 'Please'. |
| SAM | Fine, I'll get mine then. |
| | So… you got any friends? |
| TOM | I moved down from Nottingham, where I did my BA, most of them are still there. |
| | Actually. |
| | I find London strange, if I'm honest. |
| SAM | What about the flatmates? |
| TOM | Spareroom.com. |
| | They're nice. |
| | I didn't realise I would be living in the living room. |
| SAM | What – you pay that much for the sofa? |

What a dick'ead.

You ever speak up and say?

| | |
|---|---|
| TOM | It's still the cheapest I could find in this area. |
| SAM | So you're not from London. |
| TOM | Who is? |
| SAM | Me. |
| TOM | Well I guessed that. |
| SAM | Born and bred and never ever left. |
| TOM | I grew up with fields and little else, I thought I loved it here but actually I think it's really shit. |

It's all really up its arse, even here.

| | |
|---|---|
| SAM | It is what it is. |
| TOM | You should come and see how it can be – just space, just green. |
| SAM | We have that, we have lots of that. |
| TOM | You all think you have so much, but you're being lied to. |

You have no idea.

| | |
|---|---|
| SAM | Yeah well, you're all still here, so – |
| TOM | How old are you? |
| SAM | You can't tell? |
| TOM | Anywhere between seventeen and thirty-five you could be – |

Sorry.

SAM     Thanks, that's um, upsetting actually.

I'm twenty-five.

Shocked or delighted?

TOM     I'm twenty-four so yeah, same-ish age.

And yet –

| | |
|---|---|
| SAM | And yet – |
| TOM | Sorry I thought you just seemed like so many different ages. |
| SAM | I gettit. |
| TOM | What with two kids – |
| SAM | No really who are they then? |
| | Mica and Jordan by the way. |
| TOM | Nice they're really great names. |
| SAM | Mica's gunna be pissed when he realises he's named after a one-hit wonder. |
| | Rob didn't realise the bloke was gay either. Used to play the song over and over – everyone else on the estate blurting out rap music and there was Rob playing Mika full volume. Sometimes we would just sit in the car, windows down and he'd blast it out. I only had Jordan then, he was all small, screwed-up face, just screaming in my arms – but put that song on and it felt like we weren't there at all… sorry / I – |
| TOM | Rob their dad? |
| SAM | Yeah, yeah he is. |
| TOM | To them both? |
| SAM | Yes. Jesus you're bad at this. |
| TOM | Do you want another? |
| SAM | Kid? |
| | I'm joking Tom, I'm taking the piss. |
| | Yeah, somewhere else though – somewhere loud. |

*Chorus*

| | |
|---|---|
| F | And Sam thinks fucks this, |
| M | and Tom thinks fuck this too |
| | – she's beautiful when she smiles and her hips seem so sharp in the silhouette of her trousers. |
| W | A neckline that he could pluck and make bowstrings out of. |
| M | He wants to pinch the skin on her cheeks and check they're not made of glass it's so translucent. |
| F | And the lights make her slightly-too-tired eyes look like ghostly pearls. |
| W | For a moment she seems godly, |
| M | a nymph, |
| F | a naiad, |
| M | and he thinks: |
| | If I could just hold her I'd be all right. |
| F | This is when we should tell them about Tom |
| W | She didn't know |
| | Why should they? |
| F | But – |
| M/W | They go dancing. |
| | CHORUS *start to hum.* |
| M | And Sam is on fire because this is the first fucking good night out in ages, and she can just dance her heels into the soles of her shoes till her toes seem to be bleeding with the sheer force of her freedom. |
| | CHORUS *sing the first verse of 'In for the Kill' by La Roux.* |

| SAM | I'm loving this. |
| TOM | I love you too. |
| SAM | I can't hear you? |
| TOM | I said I love you too. |
| SAM | Sorry I / can't? |
| TOM | You're beautiful you know that, you're like something out of a I dunno, a fairytale. |
| SAM | Ha what, Wicked Witch of the West, mate, you're like something from another time you are, you don't seem right at all. |

*Chorus*

| W | And even though Tom thought that was the moment to kiss her – |
| | She's ruined it. |
| M | And a small part of his hard heart feels a pinprick of fucking dangerous proportions because how fucking dare she ruin his chances. |
| | CHORUS *sing the refrain of 'In for the Kill'.* |

| TOM | Do you want to go home? |
| SAM | No I want to go somewhere else, somewhere green. |
| TOM | And you're sure? |
| SAM | They're fine. People think kids are really fragile but trust me they're weirdly, I dunno, strong about everything, they just take it – in a way they're better before they've learnt about the shit. They're like goldfish with fists. |
| TOM | I thought you said they were with Rob? |
| | Sam are they at home, alone? |

*Chorus*

| | |
|---|---|
| W | Are they, Sam? |
| | Sam |
| M | Have you left them? |
| F | Sam? |
| M | Sam? |
| W | Sam takes him to the reservoir in Nunhead. |
| M | Tom has never been and it is high up and dark but there is the usual hum of London lights in the air and this is it |
| F | Tom thinks: |
| M | The moment to kiss her |
| F | But Sam is lost in the rapture of not him, but the feeling of being past the rules of her own kingdom. |
| W | Tom leans in and Sam reels at his smell – which is something like a warning sign – a sign of the rot inside. |
| F | But it's just dark enough that Sam can sort of pretend he is someone else, |
| M | and she wishes for a second that it was Rob. |
| F | But for even longer she wishes it was just her. |
| | By herself. |
| | Enjoying the feeling of air around her solitary legs and the whole world would just keep her there and hold her up without her even having to try and stand. |
| | And she could be like the grass beneath her heels, just pressed so close to earth and land – |
| M | And Tom's hands reach in and around – |

| | |
|---|---|
| W | And she feels his fingers grab for bits of thigh and buttons and she closes her eyes and gives in. |
| F | Till she remembers that she doesn't have to, if she doesn't want to. |
| | She doesn't. |

| | |
|---|---|
| SAM | Just get off yeah. |
| TOM | Why? |
| | Really? |
| SAM | Yeah. |
| TOM | But it feels exciting. |
| SAM | Yeah clearly for you. |
| | But I'm not so, just – |
| | Just back off – |
| TOM | Or what? |
| | … |
| | You're cold. |
| | Let's go home. |

*Chorus*

| | |
|---|---|
| M | The night bus feels frozen in Day-Glo orange, and neither speaks for what feels like ages. Sam is numb as she follows him up the stairs to his flat, she didn't even realise he was leading her up there. |
| W | The alcohol is starting to creep down to her fingernails, and every time she stops walking she stumbles on her arches. |
| F | At the door of his flat he gestures for her to join him – and she doesn't think she should go in – not after what just nearly happened… |

| | |
|---|---|
| W | Except she does, she very much does |
| M | Because it's been ages for fuck's sake and Sam doesn't like sleeping on her sofa all alone in her flat, |
| F | she doesn't want to spend another evening in her own skin |

– she'd rather wear someone else's right now.

CHORUS *sing the first verse of 'In for the Kill'.*

In the morning, she creeps back down to her own front door.

She flies down each flight of stairs like it's golden.

| | |
|---|---|
| M | One more broken step and she's free |

She gets in her flat and she is sick in the kitchen.

CHORUS *start to hum 'Get Free'.*

| | |
|---|---|
| W | Sam could howl like a wolf child but it would frighten her cubs |

And she thinks better to not think at all actually.

That's the best way for everyone.

| | |
|---|---|
| M | Nothing happened, did it? |
| F | Didn't it? |
| W | Nothing at all |
| SAM | Just be quiet please, just shut up, please just… just… |

CHORUS *sing the first refrain of 'Get Free'.*

| | |
|---|---|
| BOSS (W) | Late, rude to clients, attitude – the list goes on. |
| SAM | So you're firing me? |
| | You're firing me? |
| | I've got two kids, I've only been here five / fucking minutes – |
| BOSS | As I said we've had a number of complaints now Sam and you didn't show up this morning did you – 5 a.m. and you get back in time to take the kids to school, that's how this works – that's three times now Sam. You know I've tried to help you – |
| SAM | Complaints about my – |
| BOSS | Attitude yes, 'she makes a face when she cleans' – |
| SAM | I make a face when I scrub the shit out of their toilets? |
| BOSS | I have tried to warn you, Sam. |
| SAM | How am I supposed to feed them? |
| | My kids, how am I supposed / to |
| BOSS | You should've thought about that really – before you went and, what, got pissed last night was it? – I can smell it from here by the way. |
| | Look, I've got three, Sam, three under six. So don't try and make me feel guilty. I'm coping. I'm making it work. So should you. |

*Chorus*

| | |
|---|---|
| F | And in Sam's head the whole world shouts: |
| M | Fucking scum, fucking piece of nasty little scum on our streets with her screaming kids on my bus, on our streets, scrounging, nothing but a scrounger on my purse strings. |

Hanging there like some piece of white-trash
filth, like some little fucked-up slag making
accusations that she has mouths to feed.

Please.

Look don't have 'em.

If you can't look after them.

Don't fucking have 'em.

Jesus.

W          Sam's breathing is shallow as she goes back
           to her flat and she sits in stone-still silence
           till she hears the music pounding above her
           like lightning and she wishes it could gobble
           her whole.

           CHORUS *arrange the beat of 'What's a Girl
           To Do?' by Bat for Lashes, louder and louder.*

           SAM *screams at the ceiling.*

           *All sound cuts.*


TOM        I thought you were out.

SAM        You know I'm in, I'm always in. It's bed and
           bath time. That's a time when parents have to
           do a lot of shit, so shut the fucking music off.

TOM        You don't need to cry about it. Calm down.

SAM        No, no I'm not crying. I'm just.

TOM        Were you stealing earlier – in Khan's, I think
           I saw you. You were pocketing stuff.

           I almost said hello. But I didn't want to – you
           know distract you.

           You haven't texted me back. After the other
           night.

           I thought you might want another drink...

SAM        I don't / want

| | |
|---|---|
| TOM | Do you want to clean my flat, our flat? |
| | We're still looking for someone. |
| | It's cash-in-hand. If that helps? |
| SAM | … |
| | Okay. Yes, I'll do it. |
| TOM | Great, start on Sunday maybe. And I'll try and turn down the music. |
| | Hey Sam, I had fun the other night, I really enjoyed it. |

*Chorus*

| | |
|---|---|
| W | It's been three weeks since Sam started cleaning Tom's flat |
| F | And it does help, before you ask her to explain herself, in fact it makes all the difference in the world. |
| M | Because Sam might still feel uneasy when she sleeps, knowing he sleeps above her. |
| | And what happened |
| W | Didn't happen |
| F | Did happen |
| W | After the reservoir might play like a bad song over and over – but then again – how many times has Sam let someone touch her? |
| F | 'Let' / someone? |
| W | Someone she wasn't sure she liked |
| | Because they made her smile. |
| M | Because they told her for one night they'd look after her. |
| | Here is an offer – and here is safety, for a moment, for her children, for her. |

| | |
|---|---|
| F | For one more day of surviving till she can... |
| | Till she can... |
| | Till she can... |
| | |
| SAM | Library? |
| TOM | I'm not going to the library – You been – it's not quiet there at all – fucking lawless and it's just DVDs. |
| SAM | Lecture? |
| TOM | Hardly. |
| SAM | Right so you're paying for what exactly? |
| TOM | I'm not even paying so joke's on you. |
| SAM | Yeah I feel it. |
| | My sides are literally splitting. |
| | Move your feet then. |
| | You got cash to pay me? |
| TOM | Why don't you sit with me on the sofa for a bit? |
| SAM | I'm at work. |
| TOM | Hardly. |
| | We can watch TV like you wanted. |
| SAM | Right, well I think I'm done here actually. |
| TOM | You having a laugh – place is still filthy if you ask me. |
| SAM | You did that on purpose, don't add to it, / just |
| TOM | That's right pick it up... |
| | get on your knees. |
| SAM | Tom move your feet, Tom, move them, this isn't funny. |

| TOM | I think it is, I think it's hysterical, I might even YouTube it, you would be a hit on some of those websites – you should try it, then maybe you could afford to look nice, do something good for the kids. You gotta think about them after all. |
| SAM | Wow, I'm leaving. |
| TOM | Jesus, I'm only joking, Sam, anyway, I haven't paid you yet. |
| SAM | It's fifty all together. |
| TOM | No I think it's more like sixty if you sit here. |

*Chorus*

| F | Sam starts to feel like she's lost her footing in this setting – |
|   | Like she's slipping in quicksand and she's not quite sure when that happened. |
|   | Sam starts to feel like she might be dribbling – |
|   | Because her mouth isn't working properly and her brain can't seem to tell her what to do any more. |
| W | Tom has taken the reins of Sam's soul and Sam's confidence because every time she lets him touch her – |
| M | She gets an extra tenner. |
| W | And she wonders when she put a price on herself. |
| F | And as her ears buzz and her mouth gasps for words that escape her. |
|   | She sees herself shrinking so far from her own skin. |
| W | She's not even here any more. |

| F | Like a goldfish with limp fists, Sam goes limp-wristed and gives in. |
|---|---|
| W | Tom's mouth is wishy washy and he has clumsy fingers like teenage gropes it gives her shivers. |
| F | And it feels like his hands go on for far too long and she just stiffens. |

| SAM | Stop. |
|---|---|
| | I gotta go pick kids up. |
| TOM | But you haven't finished – |
| SAM | Move. Please. I need to get my children. Just. Move. |
| TOM | Whoa Sam… |
| | I don't understand. |
| | I'm just trying to help you here. |
| | I'm just trying to / help. |
| SAM | Please – |

*Chorus*

| W | And that word just over and over like pinpricks on blisters. She's stripping skin off with her teeth in her head she screams. |
|---|---|
| F | Stop it, stop. |
| | Stop this. |
| | Please |
| | Can we just? |
| | I don't want to see this bit – |

| | |
|---|---|
| ROB (M) | You called me fifteen times Sam, Carly's worried about the boys, she thinks you've gone off yer head. And I can't have her worrying, not in the state she's in. |
| SAM | I'm sorry I, just – |
| ROB | Come on, Sam, tell me what this is about and maybe we can sort it yeah, but Carly's got pregnant pilates in half an hour so we need to get moving. |
| SAM | Have you chosen it yet? |
| | The name, it was, you weren't sure last time I saw you. |
| ROB | Let's not talk about that eh, Sam. |
| SAM | It's a girl isn't it? That will balance things out a bit. Lucky really. |
| ROB | Is this about the boys Sam – are they all right? Because Carly and I are gunna need some space and time when the baby comes. I thought we'd talked about this. |
| SAM | Did you need any of the boys' old things, we kept a few bits – maybe just Babygros and – |
| ROB | – No she's bought everything new, dead excited, and all pink – you know, because it's a girl. |
| | Come on, Sam. |
| | I'm going to have to go in a minute. |
| | You're all right aren't you – yeah? |
| | We did agree that you wouldn't ask for any money. |
| | Just until we're on our feet yeah. |
| | Just until we've sorted a few things. |
| SAM | Yeah, no, that's... |
| | There's this, um, there's this guy – |

ROB          Knew it, there always is, Sam – how many
             times did you cheat on me again?

SAM          No it's / not

ROB          And what, he doesn't want the kids around
             does he? Sam come on, love, you know we
             can't take them at the moment, Carly needs
             this to be perfect. Fresh start for me. You
             understand that don't you Sam. I thought we
             were still friends. I thought you'd be happy
             for me. Look I've got to –


*Chorus*

W            Her Argonaut, the one she bore her boys for,
             leaves via the front door, a pat on the
             shoulder, a kiss on the cheek.

F            And Sam doesn't move.

             She simply sits on the pavement and stops still.

M            Just for a minute.

W            Or three, or five.

F            Until she's on autopilot and she can't run
             fast enough away and away and away and
             it's dark by the time that she makes it back
             to the flat and she can't even remember how
             she got there.


TOM          Hello Sam.

SAM          What are you doing?

TOM          The boys, you left them down here, alone,
             I just thought I'd check on them

SAM          What?

TOM          Went in just to check they were okay, asleep.

SAM          Sorry you went in my flat?

TOM          You left the door open Sam.

| SAM | You went into my – |
|-----|---|
| TOM | Leaving two little kids like that. |
| | And not for the first time. I noticed. |
| | Think I have enough to call Social Services really, could even call the / police. |
| SAM | Okay Tom, I need you to go / now. |
| TOM | Was that Rob, Sam? Was that their big strong bloke of a dad? Their big stupid-faced, ugly chav of a dad. Is that who he was? Really, he was your fucking Rob. The one you cry yourself to sleep over. Sad. Nice cheap trainers. Classy. Does he always wear his Sports Direct uniform out – does he? Sam. |

*Chorus*

| F | And she moves past him because this conversation is over |
|---|---|
| M | This guy is a freak – |
| | – And if he's fucking touched them. |
| F | She feels like ants are crawling up her throat |
| W | She gets in her door and before she can scream |
| | Jordan is standing there, pyjamas wet and sodden |
| | And they both look as sorry as each other. |

| TOM | You can't just shut me out Sam. |
|-----|---|
| | I think if you just realised that I could be the one for you, it wouldn't have to get complicated. |
| | It could be really, really easy. |
| | If you just let me. |

*Chorus*

CHORUS *arrange music of 'What's a Girl To Do?'*

| | |
|---|---|
| W | Tom says maybe they can come to an arrangement and he won't call the Social on Sam. |
| F | 'Arrangement'? |
| | He can't even say what he means. |
| W | But you can see him thinking it. |
| | And his eyes are so steely they make you think of dead fishes. |
| M | Why did she let this happen – why did she let any of this in? |
| F | She didn't mean / to |
| W | And it creeps round her house like mould and it settles on her skin like damp and she feels it when she steps on the slime that he has left on her carpet – the stench of him in her living room, |
| M | on her sofa |
| W | – her bed. |
| F | She wants to wash the whole house clean then, so she gets her gloves on and scrubs. |
| M | And then the music starts, softly at first, then louder and louder till the whole ceiling is shaking and it's his way of saying 'I have won this'. |
| W | And Sam feels the rage boil in her arms, the way life continues to throw her into the way of harm and she can't stand it any more – |
| | But she can't go and tell him off |
| | Because she can't see his smug smile one more time. |

F                   So she sits on the floor begging him to be
                    quiet, fists ready to thump and rave but Sam
                    has no strength left to lift a finger, she knows
                    she can't say a word.

                    So she puts music on instead – and she lets
                    her fight be sung at the top of her lungs.

                    CHORUS *break into full song, louder and*
                    *angrier this time. They sing the refrain of*
                    *'What's a Girl To Do?'*

POLICE (M)          You see that's not what he says, not what
                    most of the block says actually.

                    Called us a fair few times – antisocial
                    behaviour. Mess. Noise. Makes you sound
                    like a right nightmare.

SAM                 Sorry – what, but I / don't

POLICE              Never easy though is it – neighbours, all of us
                    on top of one another. Especially with kids.
                    Toddlers and students, eh, not a great mix.

                    I mean have you reported it to the council?
                    If it's past ten, I think it's 10 p.m. you can
                    complain, officially, but I'm afraid you sort
                    of have to ring a couple of times. I've got
                    teenagers. Wish I could complain about their
                    music sometimes.

                    I mean has he got physical this neighbour of
                    yours, is he aggressive. Has he actually done
                    anything physically harmful?

SAM                 He… no, no, he's never done anything
                    harmful.

F                   But / he

POLICE              Right well, um, is there anything more…

                    You see I can't really help you here.

                    Sounds like there's been a bit of a
                    misunderstanding perhaps.

Some people are just a bit, well, bit of a nuisance really.

You call that council – but just make sure you record it or something.

It's your word against his at the moment.

I mean they'll try and help.

God knows they can be a bit useless. I think everyone's just tired.

| SAM | Tired, yeah. |

*Chorus*

| W | Sam is so |
| | So |
| F | Tired. |

| TOM | Nice-looking school. |
| SAM | They won't let strangers collect them – so I think you should go – |
| | You look like a bit of a paedo. |
| TOM | Sticks and stones eh. |
| SAM | Just leave yeah. |
| TOM | No I'll walk you all home. |
| | Remember me, boys – |
| | You know who I am? |
| SAM | This is getting out of hand now Tom. |
| | What do you want from me? |
| TOM | Just to see you, thought you liked seeing me. |
| | Or were you just teasing? |
| | Were you just being a right old pricktease? |

Let's see how long till you drop down to your
fucking knees. You little fucking tease.

SAM     You broke the rules Tom, you called the
        police. Think this arrangement is off then
        actually.

TOM     Wasn't even me though was it, Sam – see
        you're even more of a risk than you realise.


*Chorus*

W       Ten months ago Sam hit Mica so hard in a
        supermarket he bit his tongue and the blood
        went everywhere.

M       Two years ago Sam grabbed Jordan's arm so
        roughly on a bus the driver started shouting at
        her and they had to get off.

W       Three weeks ago Mica cried so hard he
        started choking and Sam didn't spring into
        action like most mothers would. For a second
        she just stood there and thought – good.

F       Why are you looking at her like that?

        It wasn't. It was an accident.

        He fell

SAM     He's clumsy that one

F       Two boys – they

F/SAM   fight all the time

F       It's just, they were just

SAM     Clumsy that one.

        CHORUS *arrange music to 'Daniel' by Bat
        for Lashes*.

W       Sam has been on a watch list since the boys
        arrived, in a way she's been just a name on
        a list since the day she was born, and whilst

|   | she has never strayed too far she has most definitely gone overboard once or twice and all it takes is one more time. |
|---|---|
| M | Tom follows her and the boys all the way home from school that day and like a fucked-up Orpheus and Eurydice she doesn't dare look round in case he drags her right back into the underworld. |
| W | Sam's story is fragile and she wonders just how Tom realised this – how did he see through her and know that she was just plain vulnerable? |
| M | Like a soft-centred chew toy she's leaking at the edges and he seems to be oh so ready to show everyone the pieces. |
| W | We're showing you the pieces. |

CHORUS *sing the first verse of 'Daniel'.*


| FRIEND (F) | Alright missy, long time no see. |
|---|---|
|  | Oi it's not that much of a reunion, you gonna stop crying or what? |
|  | You big softy, you big daft cunt. |
| SAM | I, I thought you wouldn't – |
| FRIEND | What? Come round after how long, Sam, well that one wasn't born yet so what, four years – well you only shagged my boyfriend five times so I think considering he was a bit shit in bed, I've given you the silent treatment long enough. |
|  | Shall we take the boys out then or what – I'm thinking we get some cans stick 'em in the pram and get wankered by the seaside – |
|  | You in? |
| SAM | I'm, thank you, just thank you. |

| | |
|---|---|
| FRIEND | Yeah well – I stole the car off this Tinder minger and every once in a while he tries to get it back but we end up having a shag and I drive off again. |
| | Come on – |
| SAM | I haven't been outside in a while. |
| FRIEND | I can tell, the place stinks of fucking rot and piss, mate. |
| | You potty-trained 'em? |
| SAM | They get scared at night, they, they wet the bed. |
| FRIEND | Who's the bloke by the way, waving at you from the curtains? |
| | Like a proper nanna. |
| SAM | Can we just drive please? |
| FRIEND | Come on then, boys, let's go seaside. |
| | Fucking hell the air is just nicer ain't it, I swear it just taste of salt and seaweed, like a Japanese restaurant this air is. |
| | I love it. |
| | You need to stop crying, Sam. |
| SAM | I'm sorry about what I did. |
| FRIEND | We were going to get married Sam, so in a way I think you did me a favour, maybe. |
| SAM | It was still a shit thing to do. |
| FRIEND | Yeah it was, Sam, mostly because you gave him chlamydia which he then gave to me. I can't have kids Sam, thanks to you, thanks to you being the dirty little bitch that my mum said you were, she used to hate me bringing you home after school, 'kids in care always bring extra germs', either that or they steal from you, you never took anything but some bleach – you wanted to be able to clean your |

room at the home. My mum loved that story –
she used to have a right laugh over that.

So I forgive you Sam because for now that
suits me fine, but when I really think about it,
I hate you.

I hate you so much.

SAM            Do you ever just think you could jump and
               swim away, or just sink to the bottom and
               hide, just lie there and hide whilst the tide
               washed over you.

FRIEND         Stop it Sam, the boys'll see yer.

SAM            I could take them with me, we could live at
               the bottom together.

FRIEND         No more now, come on, come down, Sam.

               Take my hand Sam, please.

               I think we've said enough, Sam.

SAM            I'll see you soon yeah, maybe.

FRIEND         I think it best we wait another four years
               don't you.

SAM            He won't leave me alone.

FRIEND         Yeah I know, Sam, all the boys wouldn't
               leave you alone would they – or was it the
               other way around?

               Just concentrate on your kids, Sam, they look
               tired. They don't seem happy at all.

TOM            You haven't shown up for work.

SAM            One of the boys is ill so I couldn't.

TOM            You should let your employer know that
               really – just rude otherwise. I might start to
               think you were avoiding me.

SAM            Sorry but how long have you been sat here
               waiting?

TOM            What makes you think I've been doing that?

| | |
|---|---|
| SAM | Oh for fuck's sake Tom this is getting stupid. |
| TOM | Sorry who's stupid? |
| SAM | Not stupid, just could / you |
| TOM | Maybe you should call someone, tell them. |
| | But I think I heard you hit them the other night, I did, didn't I, I heard screaming and the things you were calling them. |
| | It was really shocking, heartbreaking. |
| SAM | You can't just make shit up, Tom. |
| TOM | Make what up? |
| | You need help Sam. |
| | You need help for that paranoid head of yours. |
| SAM | I'm going to call Rob, I'm going to get him over here. He's going to do your face in. |
| TOM | You know he can't, Sam, what's Carly's due date again? They'll be at home with their nice new baby in their nice new better family. Likes a pint doesn't he, Rob, funny, such a cliché when I think about it really. |
| SAM | This needs to stop now Tom. |
| TOM | When you think about it, you are so small Sam, you are just one tiny person on this planet that will just keep spinning, even if you're not on it. |
| | The kids can come and watch telly, if you like, if they're poorly. I could look after them. |
| | I could give them a break – from you. |

*Chorus*

CHORUS *clap the beat of 'Daniel'.*

| | |
|---|---|
| W | It has been three months since the night on Nunhead reservoir but for Sam it feels like a lifetime. |
| F | Every time Sam takes the kids to school, Tom is there waiting |
| | And so she decides to stop going. |
| W | Every time Sam tries to talk to Becca, Tom intervenes, and the other flatmate, the goofy one with the kind smile, well he doesn't even stop to shine that kind smile at her any more. |
| M | Tom's told them that she beats the kids. |
| W | And sure enough there are bruises on Mica's skin and she can't remember how he got them. |
| M | Did she put them there? |
| F | She didn't – honest he fell |
| | I saw him, he was climbing |
| SAM | He bumps into things |
| F | He does |
| SAM | He's a monkey that one |
| F/SAM | He fell |
| SAM | His brother and him they just – |
| F | Why are you looking at her like that? |
| | Stop. |
| | You're letting them / think. |
| | FURY *gives up protesting, she gives up…* |
| M | Trapped in her own head Sam comes close to madness. |
| | And her boys have stopped crying. |

W                    Because she's stopped answering.

M                    And whilst the music keeps playing

W                    they sit in silence.

                     CHORUS *sing the last verse and refrain
                     from 'Daniel'.*


SAM                  (*To us.*) Sometimes, when he plays music it
                     feels like the whole ceiling is shaking, like the
                     weight of all that sound is pushing down on
                     the foundations. Heavy. His body seeping
                     through the floorboards.

                     It even looks like it's becoming baggy.
                     Drooping like flaps of skin, like pants on
                     a washing line. My mum's face wipes against
                     a bathroom sink. I remember flashes of her
                     face, but it's just a big blur of make-up.
                     It smells like tissue paper. It smells like the hair
                     on my boys' heads at night, when I kiss them
                     in their sleep. Little moments where all I want
                     to do is hold them so tight because they're
                     perfect then. They're perfect in their stillness
                     and the world in their heads is welcoming and
                     warm and kind. And every snatched moment
                     of sleep is a good thing for them. I wish I could
                     sleep like that. I just watch them, jealous.
                     I watch them with love and disgust on my face.
                     Like she did.

                     You see the ceiling will fall in and kill us.
                     In the night, when they are sleeping. The
                     whole thing will fall down and take me with
                     it. Just down and down and deeper into the
                     ground. I think I'd like to be there.

                     It's all coming in on us and we can't keep
                     holding it up. I can't love them any more than
                     I do, and it's not very much. I'm sorry. Do
                     you believe me? Mum. I said I'm sorry, even
                     though you're the one that left me.

OFFICER 1 (W)   Hello Sam, can I come in please?

SAM             I didn't know you were coming today.

OFFICER 2 (M)   I think that's because you've been ignoring our calls.

SAM             Okay, er, yes, um I can't make you a cup of tea, I had everything capped when I was fired and they're trying to sort it but it's going to take a / while –

OFFICER 3 (F)   That's what we're here about really, Sam, you see we've had some complaints –

SAM             I've complained yes.

OFFICER 1       No against you, I'm afraid, some rather difficult accusations.

OFFICER 2       Are the boys around at all?

SAM             They're just in their bedroom.

OFFICER 1       You have the two boys sharing one room, they're how old now?

OFFICER 3       Do they want to come out and say hello?

SAM             I'll go get them.

OFFICER 1       Actually perhaps we better discuss this complaint first away from tiny ears, they pick up so much don't they –

OFFICER 2       – like parrots.

OFFICER 3       Maybe we should sit down?

SAM             There's only the sofa, which is also my bed, so just move the...

OFFICER 2       I've just bought a sofa bed from Ikea, it's called Lugnvik – how fun is that.

                It sort of makes it all the more personal.

OFFICER 1       This complaint Samantha, sorry Sam –

| | |
|---|---|
| OFFICER 2 | We've got a few Sams, Sammys and Samanthas... |
| OFFICER 3 | Are you okay Sam, your hands are um grasping... |
| SAM | Just cramp. |
| OFFICER 3 | Because you've been working? |
| SAM | No, no I'm not currently employed which is why you've stopped / my |
| OFFICER 1 | Right, see, Sam we've been notified that you have been working and not declaring it. |
| OFFICER 2 | Also Sam we understand there have been some – |
| OFFICER 3 | How do we put this – |
| OFFICER 1 | – noises coming from this flat suggesting a type of work we're not too happy with knowing that you have children living on the premises. |
| OFFICER 2 | Not happy with at all in fact Samantha. |
| SAM | Are you being serious, are you, sorry is this, um, is / this |
| OFFICER 3 | Your hands are really sort of twitching now Sam, I think you should see someone about that. |
| SAM | I, sorry who – oh God he, right yeah, okay I want to make a complaint that my, that he, that fucking, he's been saying he, he's lying basically, he's turning, it's part of his plan. I think that's what they do they sort of make everyone think that they're right and you're wrong. |
| OFFICER 1 | Okay you don't seem to be making much sense now Samantha, who is this he you're talking about? |

OFFICER 2    Is that Rob Jones their father? I understand he isn't living here currently...

SAM    No he hasn't lived here for three years, a year after Mica was born. He lives with her – Carly – in the Myatts Estate because, well, they've been saving up to buy somewhere else, a real place, somewhere with a garden, she has this job, she even wears a suit to it, she has a car, the company car, she's on maternity leave because she's pregnant you see and her brother, he, he got her the job. No I don't mean Rob, he hasn't lived here for three fucking years. I live here with them. I look after them. She's protected from all this. I – he's lying basically, this is what they do, please believe me. / He –

OFFICER 2    We don't need to know all of this, Sam. We don't want to know any of this.

OFFICER 1    We just need to focus on these rather serious allegations. Let's speak to the boys now should we?

OFFICER 3    Let's just see what they have to say.

SAM    I, I, they, I never, you can't you can't you can't just take them from me.

    Please –

    Please –


*Chorus*

W    When the social worker finally leaves

M    Or is it the key worker?

W    Or the child protection officer?

F    Sam can't breathe

    She knows that this time, this time it's happening for real and she's seething.

|  | Blood pounding in her ears with fury so hot she feels like she's burning. |
| M | Because without them she has nothing. |
| W | And she doesn't know if that's what she really wants. |

| SAM | Stop screaming, stop screaming, please be quiet why won't you be quiet? |
|  | That's why they think this, because of you, they think this because of you – |
|  | Just shut up just shut up. |

*Chorus*

| W | And she flips it, |
| M | she hits Jordan, |
| F | just once, |
| W | squarely and suddenly, and then both of them are quiet and Sam is shocked by her own hands. |
| F | How did they do that? |
|  | They won't stop shaking. |
| W | She runs then, she runs out of the house like she has done so many times before, but this time it feels different. This time she doesn't think she'll stop. |
| M | She runs so hard and so fast through the little grey streets that surround her, like a terrier on a leash, she doubles back on herself jerking at every car that goes past till she almost starts barking. |
| W | At a green light she runs across the road and nearly gets run over and she hopes she wasn't doing it on purpose. |

| | |
|---|---|
| F | Not quite, she hasn't quite given in just yet. |
| W | But she nearly has – |
| F | which is why, I think we should. Let me help her, please. I don't understand. |
| W | What don't you get? |
| M | Just watch. |
| W | Just look at her run and run and run away from the man she put herself in front of. |
| F | But she didn't, / she |
| W | Where are your kids Sam? |
| | Sam? |
| M | Have you left them? |
| W | Have you Sam? |
| | Sam? |
| F | Sam looks London in the eye, as rain starts to fall from a tepid summer sky and she knows that even though she could keep on running, she's not ready to leave them. |
| W | Sam goes back to her flat, |
| M | but when she gets through her front door – her boys aren't waiting for her. They're not there at all. |
| SAM | Mica? |
| | Jordan? |

*Chorus*

| | |
|---|---|
| W | And then she hears them – coming from his flat, cartoons, laughter. |
| M | The sound of her son's small feet flitting floorboards above her. |

F                    And she feels the bile rise in her throat then
                     till it burns so hard she could be choking

                     Because it certainly doesn't feel like she's
                     breathing

SAM                  Tom –

                     Tom –

                     Let me in, Tom –

                     Fucking let me in.

                     Tom.

                     Let me in or I'll call the fucking police, TOM.

TOM                  Shhh, hello Sam.

                     They're watching telly aren't you, boys.

                     Does Mummy want to watch it with us?

                     Come on, Sam, they want you to play along.

                     Well stop standing there like some fucking
                     idiot Sam and sit down like I told you to.


*Chorus*

F                    Sam sits down.

                     And whilst her boys snuggle close to her, she
                     can barely move for fear of what is coming
                     next because none of this makes any sense.

W                    But nothing happens.

                     He doesn't lay a finger on her.

M                    He just makes her a cup of tea

                     And pretends for a bit that he can be the
                     perfect boyfriend.

W                    Until his flat begins to close in on her and it is
                     like they are playing a horrible game of

|   | house, and at any moment she might just break a rule. |
|---|---|
| F | Sam starts to dig her nails into her palms to stop from crying – she can't let him see her cry. |
| W | The lights outside go dark and the streetlights flicker |
|   | The boys fall asleep as the cartoons glare at them |
| M | And Tom stands behind her |
|   | Behind the sofa. |
|   | And looks down as if surveying his family |
|   | – A pride of sleeping lions. |

TOM  All I wanted was this.

Just this, easy isn't it – just nice.

You don't always get this in my family.

SAM  In anyone's family Tom.

TOM  We could be so very, very happy.

You realise that don't you?

That you are it, the thing that can make it work.

If you just wanted it to.

You could make this so much easier.

SAM  No, Tom.

/ That –

TOM  No but it would Sam you don't seem / to –

SAM  The boys need their beds now Tom can we do that?

TOM   Do you think you're a good mother, Sam?
To those boys? Are they going to grow up to
be the human beings you want them to be?
Do you really love them, if so, how could you
leave them so easily Sam, how could you
scream at them?

I just don't know if you deserve them.

…

When you hurt them, grab their little arms
and pull at them, does it feel like this?

SAM   Tom you're hurting me.

TOM   Can you feel how hard this is, how much this
hurts –

Are you in pain now Sam?

Is this hurting you?

SAM   Tom you're scaring them –

TOM   No I'm scaring you.

Just like you scare them and that's why they
scream and shout all night long.

That's why I turn the music up loud to drown
you and your horrible kids out.

You're wetting yourself Sam, is that how
scared you are?

SAM   Tom, please you need / to –

TOM   No, Sam, I don't need to do anything.

See, you're not right, Sam, you're just
damaged goods, a fucking *Sun* headline.
You're nothing but a piece of fucking filth and
I don't understand why you can't see how
much better I am.

If you want them Sam, if you really want
them, then prove it.

But you see you can't can you – because you
don't have anything left. And no one needs
you to succeed at this Sam, we are all so
ready for you to fucking fail. And that is
exactly what you're doing –

You're just failing again and again and again.

You see my mum would leave me in my room
and pretend to lock the door, and I would
scream and scream to be let out and sometimes
she would sit on the other side and just laugh,
because she was, I don't know, Sam, she was
like having a bully living with you all day,
every day, and everyone was scared of her, and
I thought mums were supposed to be like they
were in books and on TV but she had these
moments Sam where she would just lash and
lash and throw herself around the house and
I thought – 'you're evil'–

SAM

Did you ever stop to think that maybe it was
you – that your mum looked at your face as
soon as you were born and thought – that's
what evil is. That's not a face I can stand.

We are not fucking superhuman Tom we
cannot be blamed for everything.

TOM

You already are.

TOM *grabs* SAM *by the throat, she tries to
push him off her – they stay suspended –
struggling.*

*Chorus*

W          Her time is running out

M          Which one is the monster?

F          Him?

M          Her?

W          Us?

| F | We need there to be a decision. |
| | Or would you rather there was just silence? |
| | Huge and hideous silence whilst you scream and scream on the inside. |
| | All day |
| | Every day |
| M | As they pass you on the street and tut at you and your children |
| | What can you really offer them? |
| W | See we can't look after anyone any more. |
| | We don't really care |
| M | And he will get away with it, because they always do |
| F | But the boys |
| | Somebody has to think of her children |
| W | Are they better off without her? |
| M | Maybe they would be better off without her. |
| W | Maybe they would be better off dead. |

SAM *lets this thought reverberate through her – and then she makes her decision.* SAM *pushes* TOM *away from her so hard he falls backwards. She picks up a chair and smashes it through the television – white noise fills the space. She picks up a shard of the broken television – and holds it out defensively.*

CHORUS *hum – the hum builds, music starts to build to the 'Get Free' chorus we heard at the beginning of the play. The world should feel like it is beginning to cave in.*

SAM *looks at* TOM, *she goes to cut him, but turns the point to her own stomach and blood pours – out of her womb and out of her mouth – the ceiling falls, perhaps* FURY *brings it down, perhaps all the* CHORUS *do, perhaps* SAM *climbs up and pulls it down herself – it crashes around* SAM. *The lights explode, the music has built to a climax, but now it stops – she is alone on stage – her world has caved in on itself.* SAM *has reached the underworld. Darkness except for a flickering light on* SAM *drenched in blood.*

SAM          Mica?

Jordan?

Where are you?

I can't see you.

…

I'm sorry.

Do you believe me?

I said, I'm sorry.

Even though I'm the one who left you.

SAM *sings or speaks the first refrain of 'Get Free'.*

*Light out.*

*End.*

**A Nick Hern Book**

*Fury* first published in Great Britain as a paperback original in 2016 by
Nick Hern Books Limited, The Glasshouse, 49a Goldhawk Road, London
W12 8QP, in association with Soho Theatre and Damsel Productions

*Fury* copyright © 2016 Phoebe Eclair-Powell

Phoebe Eclair-Powell has asserted her right to be identified as the author of
this work

Cover image: Sarah Ridgeway as Sam; photography: The Other Richard and
Colin Tonks

Designed and typeset by Nick Hern Books, London
Printed and bound in Great Britain by Mimeo Ltd, Huntingdon, Cambridgeshire
PE29 6XX

A CIP catalogue record for this book is available from the British Library

ISBN   978 1 84842 591 0

**Woodland**
**CARBON**
www.woodlandcarbon.co.uk
NICK HERN BOOKS
Printed on Carbon Captured paper